HABITATS

MW01089616

TROPICAL RAINFOREST

BY BRENNA MALONEY

Children's Press®
An imprint of Scholastic Inc.

A special thank-you to the team at the Cincinnati Zoo & Botanical Garden for their expert consultation.

Copyright © 2024 by Scholastic Inc.

All rights reserved. Published by Children's Press, an imprint of Scholastic Inc., *Publishers since 1920.* SCHOLASTIC, CHILDREN'S PRESS, and associated logos are trademarks and/or registered trademarks of Scholastic Inc.

Library of Congress Cataloging-in-Publication Data available

ISBN 978-1-339-02078-5 (library binding) / ISBN 978-1-339-02079-2 (paperback)

10 9 8 7 6 5 4 3 2   24 25 26 27 28

Printed in China   62
First edition, 2024

Book design by Kay Petronio

Photos ©: cover top and throughout: Mary Ann McDonald/Getty Images; 4-5: Robin Smith/Getty Images; 6-7: NASA; 8 center left: ToniFlap/Getty Images; 8 bottom: Yuina Takase/Getty Images; 9 center left: Peter Schoen/Getty Images; 9 center right: Patrick Boelens/Getty Images; 9 bottom: RUBA48/Getty Images; 10-11 top: Galen Rowell/Getty Images; 10-11 bottom: Carles Navarro Parcerisas/Getty Images; 12-13: Christian Vinces/Getty Images; 14-15: Juan Carlos Vindas/Getty Images; 20-21: Ondrej Prosicky/Getty Images; 24-25: Ellen Goff/DanitaDelimont/Alamy Images; 26-27: M. Watson/ardea.c/Mary Evans Picture Library/age fotostock; 30 bottom center: Asergieiev/Getty Images; 30 bottom right: Natalia Babok/Getty Images.

All other photos © Shutterstock.

SQUIRREL MONKEY

GREEN ANACONDA

CONTENTS

Welcome to the Tropical Rainforest . . 4

Where in the World? 6

Life in the Tropical Rainforest 8

Day and Night 10

DAYTIME

Jaguar 12

Toucan 14

Squirrel Monkey 16

Macaw 18

Capybara 20

NIGHTTIME

Green Anaconda 22

Aye-Aye 24

Sloth 26

Flying Fox 28

You Decide! 30

Glossary 31

Index 32

WELCOME TO THE TROPICAL RAINFOREST

Tropical rainforests are hot and wet places full of trees. It rains a lot in these forests! Most get more than 80 inches (2 m) of rain a year. Many different plants and animals call the rainforest home. You can hear the sounds of these different animals all day long.

Wake up to the loud call of macaws in the morning. Hear the chatter of squirrel monkeys during the day. Wait for the hum of insects at dusk and the croaking sounds of tree frogs at night.

Many of the items we use daily come from rainforests, including medicines, coffee, and fruits.

THREE LARGEST TROPICAL RAINFORESTS

ARCTIC

ARCTIC OCEAN

EUROPE

NORTH AMERICA

ATLANTIC OCEAN

AFRICA

PACIFIC OCEAN

EQUATOR

SOUTH AMERICA

Amazon Rainforest, South America
The largest tropical rainforest

Congo Rainforest, Africa
The second-largest tropical rainforest

SOUTHERN OCEAN

Tropical rainforests cover about six percent of Earth's surface.

FACT

ANTARCTICA

ASIA

PACIFIC OCEAN

INDIAN OCEAN

New Guinea Rainforest, Oceania
The third-largest tropical rainforest

AUSTRALIA

Tropical rainforests are found close to the **equator**. The equator is an imaginary circle around the middle of Earth. Areas along the equator receive more direct sunlight. It is hot year-round. Tropical rainforest temperatures are usually between 70° to 85°F (21° to 30°C).

7

LIFE IN THE TROPICAL RAINFOREST

TOUCAN

Tropical rainforests are full of life! There are tall trees and interesting plants such as Venus flytraps and orchids. There are also many animals! They have different ways to survive. Some are active by day.

GREEN ANACONDA

VENUS FLYTRAPS

CAPYBARAS

FLYING FOX

MACAW

SQUIRREL MONKEYS

JAGUAR

Others are **nocturnal**. They are active at night. Some are brightly colored. Their coloring warns **predators** that they will not taste good. Many use **camouflage** to keep themselves hidden.

FACT
Half of the world's plant and animal **species** live in rainforests.

EMERGENT LAYER

FOREST FLOOR

DAY AND NIGHT

Tropical rainforest temperatures do not change that much between day and night. Most rainforests have four layers. The emergent layer is at the top. During the day it receives the most sunlight and wind. The middle layers are called the canopy and understory. The forest floor is at the bottom. The thick tree branches and leaves block most of the sunlight and wind. It is darker, **humid**, and less windy there both during the day and at night. What do animals do as the days go by? Read on to find out!

JAGUAR

A jaguar starts hunting before dawn. It hides among the leaves and trees while it looks for **prey**. Padded paws help it move silently. Soon this **carnivore** spots a turtle in the river. Jaguars are excellent swimmers. Their teeth are strong enough to bite through a turtle's hard shell. The jaguar slips into the water to eat.

FACT A jaguar's tongue is rough like sandpaper.

Toucans make a lot of noises! They grunt, snore, and croak like frogs. **FACT**

TOUCAN

It is still dawn in the rainforest. High above in the canopy, a toucan hops from branch to branch. Its bright colors provide camouflage in the morning sun. The toucan is searching for fruit. These birds eat fruit that other animals can't reach. They like figs, oranges, and guavas. The saw-like edges on their beaks help them eat the fruit. Toucans also eat insects, small reptiles, and bird eggs.

SQUIRREL MONKEY

By day, squirrel monkeys can be seen in the canopy, too. These little monkeys are about the size of dolls. They like to move in groups. They are **omnivores**. They feed on fruit and insects. Good eyesight helps them spot tasty fruit among the green leaves. Their hands and fingers can hold on to food while they peel it. They eat with their sharp teeth.

FACT These mammals got their name because they are quick like squirrels.

Macaws are the world's largest parrots.

MACAW

Squirrel monkeys share the canopy with colorful macaws. In the daytime, you often hear these birds before you see them. They fill the air with their loud calls. They fly for miles to find food. Their strong toes can firmly grip tree branches. Most macaws eat seeds, nuts, and fruits. They have powerful bills. Their bills are strong enough to crack open hard-shelled foods.

CAPYBARA

A family of capybaras is spotted below the macaws on the forest floor. It's time for a dip in the river to eat. Capybaras are most active just when the sun begins to set. These mammals are strong swimmers. Their bodies are built for life in the water. Partially webbed toes help them paddle around. Their long fur dries quickly in the sun. Capybaras are **herbivores**. They eat water plants and grasses.

FACT Capybaras are the world's largest **rodents**.

GREEN ANACONDA

The sun has set. The capybara must look out for the green anaconda. These snakes spend most of their time in the water. They are nocturnal and hunt at night. Only their eyes and nostrils can be seen above water. Anacondas are **constrictors**. They wrap their bodies around their prey and squeeze. Their jaws stretch so they can swallow prey whole. After a big meal, anacondas can go weeks without eating again.

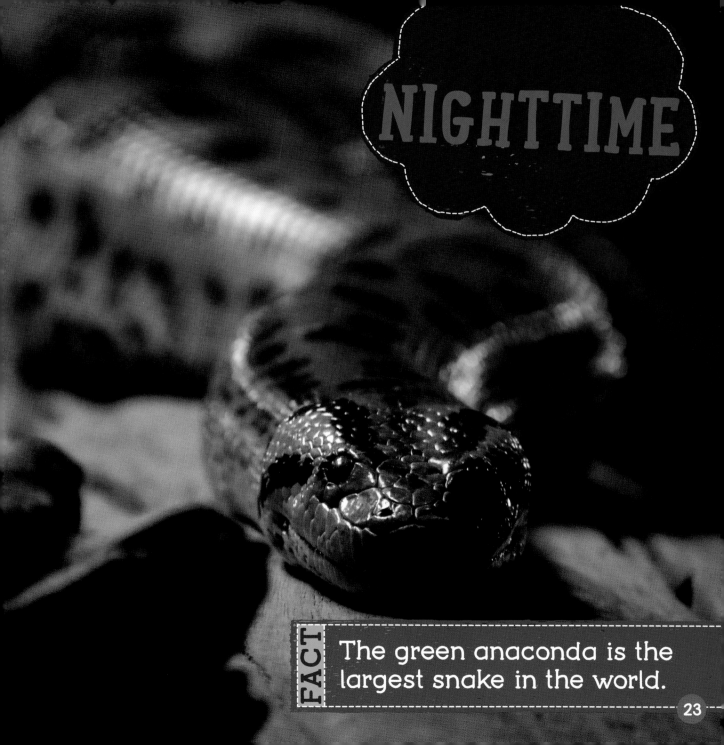

NIGHTTIME

FACT The green anaconda is the largest snake in the world.

The aye-aye has very large
eyes to help it see in the dark.

FACT

AYE-AYE

Long after the sun sets, the aye-aye wakes up to search for food. This mammal has sharp teeth. It has a long, thin middle finger and pointed claws on each fingertip. It uses these features to hunt in an unusual way. The aye-aye will tap on trees to locate **grubs**. Once its sensitive ears pick up a **hollow** sound, the aye-aye chews a hole into the wood. It pushes its long finger into the tree, hooks the grub with its sharp nail, and pulls it out to eat.

SLOTH

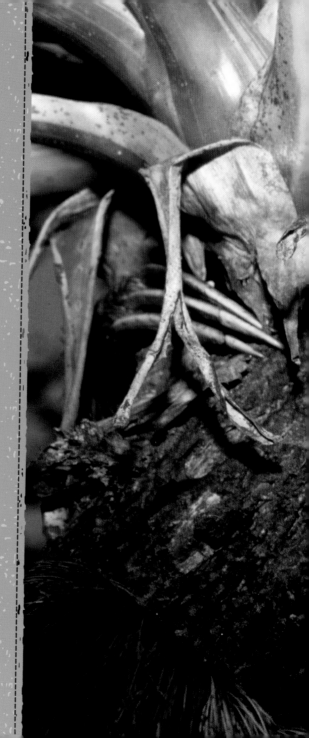

Rainforest sloths are active at night. But it can be hard to tell! These sluggish animals don't move very much or very quickly. They spend most of their lives hanging upside down from trees. Their hooked claws and long arms let them hang even while they are asleep. Sloths eat leaves, twigs, and buds. They only go to the bathroom about once a week!

FACT It's common for algae to grow on a sloth's fur. This helps camouflage it.

To cool down, flying foxes skim across rivers to wet their stomachs. This is called a belly dip.

FACT

FLYING FOX

Flying foxes also work the night shift. They are the largest members of the bat family. They roost, or rest, in trees during the day in big groups. At night, they feed on nectar, pollen, and fruit. That is why these mammals are also known as fruit bats. Flying foxes might travel 19 miles (31 km) in their nightly search for food.

YOU DECIDE!

If you could choose, would you visit the tropical rainforest during the day or at night? If you go during the day, wear your sunscreen and climb a tree! The lower you are, the darker it gets. If you are daring enough to explore the rainforest at night, bring your flashlight. A lot of animals start their day after the sun sets. At home, you can learn even more about the rainforest and the amazing animals who live there!

GLOSSARY

camouflage (KAM-uh-flahzh) to disguise something so that it blends in with its surroundings

carnivore (KAHR-nuh-vor) an animal that eats meat

constrictor (kuhn-STRIK-tur) a snake that kills by wrapping around its prey and squeezing it

equator (i-KWAY-tur) an imaginary line around the middle of Earth that is equal distance from the North and South Poles

grub the wormlike stage of some insects

herbivore (HUR-buh-vor) an animal that only eats plants

hollow (HAH-loh) empty inside

humid (HYOO-mid) weather that is moist and usually very warm

nocturnal (nahk-TUR-nuhl) active at night

omnivore (AHM-nuh-vor) an animal that eats both plants and meat

predator (PRED-uh-tur) an animal that lives by hunting other animals for food

prey (pray) an animal that is hunted by another animal for food

rodent (ROH-duhnt) a mammal with large, sharp front teeth that are constantly growing and used for gnawing things

species (SPEE-sheez) one of the groups into which animals and plants are divided

INDEX

A

Amazon Rainforest, 6, **6**
aye-aye, 24-25, **24−25**

B

beaks and bills, 15, 19
bird calls, 5, 14, 19

C

capybara, **8**, 20-21, **20−21**
claws, 25-26
Congo Rainforest, 6, **6**

D

daytime animals, 12-21
diet and eating/hunting, 12, 15-16, 19-20, 22, 25-26, 29

E

Earth, 6-7, **6−7**
emergent layer, **10−11**, 11
equator, **6−7**, 7
eyes and eyesight, 16, 24

F

fingers and toes, 16, 19-20, 25
flying fox, **9**, **28**, 28-29
forest floor, **10−11**, 11
fruit bat. *See* flying fox

G

green anaconda, **8**, 22-23, **22−23**

J

jaguar, **9**, 12-13, **13**

M

macaw, **9**, 18-19, **18−19**

N

New Guinea Rainforest, 7, **7**
nighttime animals, 22-29

O

orchids, 8

R

rainfall, 4
rainforests, 7. *See also* tropical rainforests

S

sloth, 26-27, **26−27**
squirrel monkey, **9**, 16-17, **16−17**
survival, 8-9

T

teeth, 12, 16, 22, 25
temperatures, tropical rainforest, 7
toucan, **8**, **14**, 14-15
tropical rainforests, **6−7**, **10−11**, **30**
about, 4-11
animals and plants in, 4-5, **4−5**, 8-9, **8−9**, 30
day and night in, 11
layers in, **10−11**, 11
three largest, 6-7, **6−7**

V

Venus flytraps, 8, **8**

ABOUT THE AUTHOR

Brenna Maloney is the author of dozens of books. She lives and works in Washington, DC, with her husband and two sons. She wishes she had more pages to tell you about tropical rainforests. She could never be a sloth because she moves too fast. But she wishes she could swim like a capybara.